MUSE: The Lyrics

Also by
AMANI ABDUL

Lyrics of an Angel: poetry in reality

Lions Lair

**Chasing Peace: Freeing Your Spirit and
Releasing Your Soul**

MUSE Poetry CD
www.AmaniAbdul.com
Amazon.com
iTunes
CDBaby

MUSE: The Lyrics

poetry from the spoken word CD,
MUSE.

Copyright © 2008 by Amani Abdul

ISBN 978-1-929985-08-1

Cover design by Frankie Fultz

For orders or information, write to:
info@AmaniAbdul.com

www.AmaniAbdul.com

Angel Heart Publishing

MUSE: The Lyrics

By Amani Abdul

Dedicated to the MUSES in my life-
Thank You for the inspiration, without
you my pages would be an empty
canvas.

MUSE: The Lyrics

Supermac

Intro: AK

I am your black Clark Kent
Supermac
afro shades
cruise the Lac
damn it's strong
pimp hand stronger
she came along
I had to put that on her
that Lois Lane
I got her tamed
keep her juiced up
my word seducer
Supermac
that's right
all thru the night
her love is like my
kryptonite
yes...

As I think about how I had it all figured out
you waltz about and blow me away
I think of you all day and throughout the
night
how can a man I've only seen twice six
months ago
completely blow my mind
and capture my heart

only time will define the relation to this
situation I'm in
and within the two thousand plus miles of
pure unadulterated sin
I stay in these confined walls

Has destiny called for us
or is it an unprofessed lust?
I must admit I'm intrigued
with you
by you
your smile
your vibrant, sexy style
your voice leaves me paralyzed
sending chills and waves of butterflies
through my body leavin' me breathless
completely ounceless
as you control my thoughts miles apart
and taken over my protected, cynical heart

I question motives of macness
brought by your Supermac ability
to expose my sensitivity
I stand blinded by my sensibility
that you have induced in me
Supermac, I'm so confused by you
are you real? are you Memorex?
I grow perplexed attempting to figure you
out
with no clue about your intended motives
for me
I yearn for you more and more

continuously
endlessly
timelessly
Supermac, what have you done to me?

South Beach

wow
South Beach
atmosphere
ever so clear
but
oh my
to my wondering eyes
appears
this
what was that?
i had to look back

tall, dark, handsome
smooth
only to elude
me
he retracted his steps
set his eyes into my soul
he spoke words
that set me free

we walked
we talked
for what seemed like an eternity
to find
was here
hidden behind

blowing my mind
in South Beach

i watched the moon disappear in his eyes
and felt the sun rise at his lips
he's wooing me
with this "Love Jones" poem
about being in between my thighs
as i'm swaying away at his hips

had me mesmerized with knowledge
that was symbolic to him
i wanted to scream
wake up from this wet dream
that i had fallen into
with you
on South Beach

his affection caused an
oh my...
umm umm umm
sweet mother of mine
life couldn't be so kind
love came down
and struck me blind

i felt my heart racing
a million miles a minute

all of earth and heaven
came tumbling down
i was on cloud eleven
bypassed 7, 8, 9 and even 10
standing with you then
on South Beach

Frozen Rose

How long does a Frozen Rose last?
when two people come to pass
one another
on a bright warm day
in March
remember?
the wind slightly blowing
the sun setting
sky glowing
small crowd of folks gathered
at a market place
with just a trace
of you
smiling at me
could it be? indefinitely?
Is it possible to love one and set them free?

How long does a Frozen Rose last?
when seemingly soul mates
stumble across one another
only to find
the other
leaving behind
one
up comes the sun
day two
with you
I'm blue

would it be? indefinitely?
Is it possible to love one and set them free?

How long does a Frozen Rose last?
Einstein was all too clever
to discover
that E=MC2
and now I'm
to dare
figure out
that deep within my soul
I'm left
bare…..
because of a situation
that won't ever equal the equation
due to the fact that my love
has another
it's just not fair
and this leaves me to envy
that she has
what was meant
for me to discover
should it be? indefinitely?
Is it possible to love one and set them free?

How long does a Frozen Rose last?
until the day the sun breaks through
whether I am or am not with you
never?
yet still,

I will
hold your rose frozen
until the day has passed
when our deep emotions interfere
and we are
to face
at last
what we
fear
will break us apart
forever?.!
indefinitely?
Is it possible to love one and set them free?

How

long

does

a

Frozen Rose

last?

Sleeping Cutie

Watching him as he lays down 2 sleep
I wonder…
What is it about him that has me in this
deep?
He has magic to release my inhibitions
and set my mind on fire,
I've never been an exhibitionist
but I would always want to fulfill his every
desire.

For some odd reason
that I cannot understand,
my feelings overwhelmed me
regarding this particular man.

His bright smile melts me,
his deep voice makes my day.
Through his mysterious dark eyes I saw
infinity
and within his strong muscular arms my
pains go away.

Just the gentle touch of his hand
would drive me into a craze,
his warm kisses on my forehead
would send me into a daze.

And after our breakfast
I enjoy his tight embrace,
no one has ever gotten this close to my heart

or has ever captured this place.

Within my dreams he haunts me,
in my waking moments he preoccupies my
mind.
I find myself desperately trying to break free
but for the first time I realize the meaning of
Love Is Blind.

What is it about him?
Who is he to me?
That even in my sleep I can't escape him
My Sleeping Cutie…

.

.

.

Now I lay me down to sleep
I pray the Lord my love to keep
if he should go before his spell I break
I guarantee my heart he shall forever take.

.

.

.

Sweet Dreams

.

.

.

When I First Saw Your Smile

When I First Saw Your Smile
a ray of sunshine
a glass of sparkling white wine
a full bloomed rose
that's how you got that heart of mine

Stars of a dark sky
shooting through me
but why

A sun lit underground road
with blossoms, lilies and violets
to hype the mode
When I First Saw Your Smile

When I First Saw Your Smile
precious and rare
no other can compare
as I stood there
and stare
I wonder...
who this man is
standing within my vision
eyes playing cosmic dare

a tease
to please
but from where

could he be
a sight of pure fantasy
that's a reality to me…
When I First Saw Your Smile

When I First Saw Your Smile
a walk that's danced
a spoken song
of imaginary romance
never lasts long

A tale of fairies
beauty of snow
'till when will it carry
one will never know
When I First Saw Your Smile

Muse

fine
and sweet
intelligent
and deep
he said, "Magnificent" they called him
and I could see why
he had an energy
that superseded any high
knowledge to the sky
and a heart as wide
as the ocean
had me feeling
emotions
I hadn't felt in a while
quite adorable
I found his smile
sense of humor
and style
and though we
were separated
by many miles
from where we
first met
I
just couldn't forget
him
wrote many words
together
said we'd stay

friends forever
riding high
My Muse & I

My Muse
would sing away
my blues
through silent music
that would ooze
bemuse
and infuse
me
all at once
would share with me
his views and news
and we would cruise
high
catchin' the sun
above any northern/southern sky
My Muse & I
and when I get down and low
it is to him
I go
for a quick pick me up rhyme
that would heal me
in no time
it would just fly by
My Muse & I

and though the separation

was bad
and at times
I would feel sad
that he wasn't there
I knew in my heart
he cared
so I didn't mind
knew it would be a matter of time
so I tried not to cry
for
My Muse & I.

Mr. Unforgettable

Mr. Unforgettable
yeah, that's what you are
and have been
some say it's easy to forget
that it's easy to move on
time heals all wounds
eventually life goes on
but who are they to say
to speak of you?
if only they knew
the real, super-fantastic you

Mr. Unforgettable
how fantastic you are/were
I feel your shining star
shine upon me
as if you were still here
to guide me
oh how I wish
I could bring you back
it's been so long
so many years have passed
since I saw you last
in reality
yet I'm holding on strong
with my mentality

Mr. Unforgettable
yes, unforgettable you are
as incredible you were

you continue to live in me forever
as I continue to feel your star
shining upon me still
I don't know why things turn out
the way that they do
I can't understand why
the universe took super-fantastic you
some have said that
the good ones are at times
taken too soon
so I look for you
upon the appearance of the moon

just one wish I would request
from my universal genie to grant-
it would be a blessing
to have you near me
and for a moment
my wish is granted
but it's never enough
you visit in my dreams
and at times it's tough
to see you
to talk with you
and then to awake
and find you gone
leaving me to long
for the next moment
I can see you again

Mr. Unforgettable
unbelievable you are/were

a super-fantastic man
I feel your shining star
shining upon me still
as I stand
'til this very day
in every way
protecting me, guiding me
throughout every single day
oh how I wish I could bring you back
for just one moment
even if it were stolen
just to hold you one time
and tell you just how much
I miss you
appreciate you
honor you

Mr. Unforgettable
I will always love you!

It Had To Be You

you breathe in me, fulfilling me
my energy to be me
you feel me, every part of me
my uncontrollable desire trying to be free
you instill in me the feeling
that has been lost for what seemed like an
eternity
you gave back to me that missing serenity

you see me as i am
caringly beside me you stand strong
selflessly you guide me through another
verse of life's song

you have given me hope
in each and every case
you've lifted my spirit
and sparked my days
you are my inspiration darling
in so many ways

a knight in shining armor
you have been a blessing to have
in my spiritual space
you calm my sleepless nights
and aid me through my longest of days

you've sparked the sleeping, apathetic spirit
within me

and rejuvenated my troubled soul
you've challenged me to higher limits
and helped me reinstate my stagnant goals

you are my inspiration
inspiring me to greater highs
you see the levels within me
and continuously encourage me to fly

i am grateful the universe brought us
together
a wish that it can only manifest true
you are my inspiration, darling,
It Had To Be You.

Consumed

Consumed- by the thought of you
Consumed- by the touch of you

never did I feel or even dream that I would
be here
completely naked and bare
emotions aware
my thoughts are there
with you

transparent I am
around you
without walls or boundaries
I stand before you
completely Consumed
with just you

my defenses are defenseless
as I grow Consumed
with a man I've only thought of
and eventually thinking he doesn't exist
in the midst
of so many
could have any
but none would see me for who I am
or could be
but only of what I am to the initial eye you
see

none could see through me
but you- you amaze me
reading every bit of me
what I like
what I am capable to do
I find myself falling for you

as you continue to breathe in me
I try to resume my dignity, anonymity,
sanity
in your world
and as I try to hold on
as much as I can
to my growing feelings
I find myself
imagining you
next to me as I awake this morning
kissing you ever so gently
feeling your hands caressing me tenderly
I escape in my thoughts of you
and realize that I am totally Consumed by
you.

My Fantasy

I close my eyes and fly
to the land of you
(I do this often you see)
and as I'm lying there
my body starts to quiver
at the thought of
you
and
me
as I start to shiver
to what I see
-you holding me
-gently stroking my hair
-caressing my body
-clothes barely there
I lose control
and begin to moan
uncontrollably
then I feel your hands
slowly moving down my spine
and I stop for a moment
only to rewind
and see you this time
standing behind me
your hands messaging my inner thighs
I rest the back of my head on your chest
and let out a gentle cry
as I continue to quiver a little faster
I moan a little louder

you turn me around
I look into your eyes and black out
from my emotional rush
due to my overwhelming crush
for you
(I feel like I'm in high school again)
I don't know what to do
I look at you day to day
and ponder including you
in My Fantasy to play
but end up chickening out
and blaming the universe
for it's cruel way
of a joke.

My Fantasy
My Fantasy
………….. is up in smoke.

Playing With Fire

this whole evolution
that's about to take place
can cause a revolution
and make us lose face
it can take us up
or bring us down
do you think we should stop
or shall we just drown
i can feel your touch
your smooth finger tips
oh how i want so much
to kiss your sweet lips

we're playing with fire
of pure ecstasy
take me higher
'til i just can't see
fulfill my every desire
my need to be
we're playing with fire
you and me

as i sit down
and you sit across
i look into your eyes
once again i'm lost
i see the passion
you hold so close
i'd like to get in on the action
maybe even an overdose

you hide your emotions
don't want the truth to be shown
but I've got real devotion
you won't ever have to be alone

we're playing with fire
of pure ecstasy
take me higher
'til i just can't see
fulfill my every desire
my need to be
we're playing with fire
you and me.

Whateverman

you say that you can't handle a
relation-ship
of non affirmation
you're growing my frustration
and aggravation
and you state with clarification
that you need this
you and me association
but you're driving me crazy with your
delusional stories
accusing me because of your own
insecurities
and that's a lifelong disease
and please brother please

I'm the one who sat and listened
to your ghetto girl DJ
and watched you and that wanna be female
VJ
and you're supposed to be my man
and I always have to point all this stuff out
to you
but never do you take a stand
so I end up telling you what to do
WHATEVERMAN!

you don't have any female friends
'cause you slept with them all

and is that my fault
that was your call and fall
and I really think it's sad
but now you're asking me to recall
all my male friends and all
you just can't screw everybody
then again
I guess you really don't know me
WHATEVERMAN!

yet you continuously say
that you want me to stay
but you can't understand
that I can't sway away
from my original plan
but you're supposed to be my man
and I'm supposed to support you and your
dreams
when your dreams are really your boy's
dreams
and to me it seems
that you can't even be on time for me
but for a cause you have no stake in
your there again and again and again and
again
at 7 or even 5:30
when you can't even support me
arrivin' to functions at 9, 9:30
to my events
does that make any sense?
I think not
WHATEVERMAN!

and you constantly say that you love me so
and that you don't want me to go
but you have a lot to show
and far more to grow
you're content with life
in a dinner or a movie
where as
I want
to see
to learn
to grow
but for you
life is just groo-vy

I mean let's face it
this place was never gotten
for you and me
it was a convenience for you and your boys
so that you all can work out together
and play your toys
as I stand to make silent noise
'cause of course this was not my choice
or do you remember?
WHATEVERMAN!

baby it's not you
it's me
'cause
I'm just not used to this
men-tality
with no compatibility
and I'm losing my creativity

so for my own sanity
I will have to leave
just for convenience you see

I have dreams
and plans
and ambitions
of my own
not of any other woman or man
but of me, myself, and I
alone
do you understand?
WHATEVERMAN!

well, in conclusion to thee
I
see
that we
are of 2
identity
and please, baby please
don't
you
run
that
sh!t
on
me
WHATEVERMAN!

www.ingramcontent.com/pod-product-compliance
Lightning Source LLC
Chambersburg PA
CBHW071800020426
42331CB00008B/2335